Contents

Some words are printed in bold, **like this**. You can find out what they mean on page 30. You can also look in the box at the bottom of the page where they first appear.

God of war

The Aztec people lived many years ago. They lived in an area that is now part of Mexico (see map). They ruled the area from about 1300 to the early 1500s. That is about 500 years ago.

This map shows where the Aztecs first settled. They built the city of Tenochtitlán on the western side of Lake Texcoco.

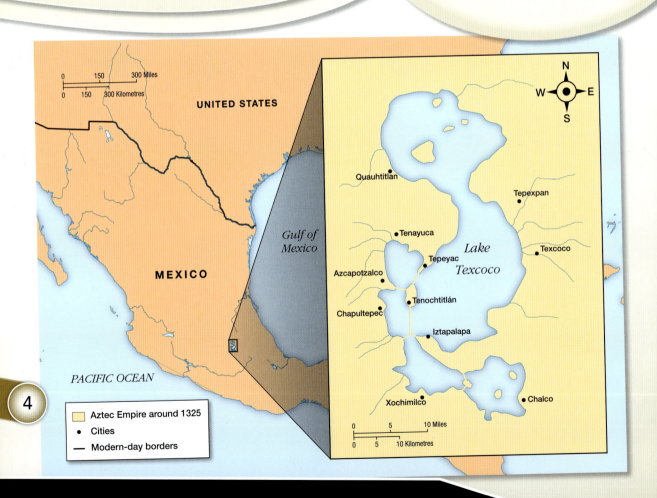

UNITED STATES

0   150   300 Miles
0   150   300 Kilometres

Gulf of Mexico

MEXICO

PACIFIC OCEAN

Aztec Empire around 1325
• Cities
— Modern-day borders

Quauhtitlan

Tepexpan

Tenayuca

Tepeyac

Lake Texcoco

Texcoco

Azcapotzalco

Tenochtitlán

Chapultepec

Iztapalapa

Xochimilco

Chalco

0   5   10 Miles
0   5   10 Kilometres

N
W   E
S

sacrifice give up or kill something, often to please a god
serpent large snake

Heidi Moore

www.raintreepublishers.co.uk
Visit our website to find out more information about **Raintree** books.

To order:
☎ Phone 44 (0) 1865 888112
📄 Send a fax to 44 (0) 1865 314091
💻 Visit the Raintree bookshop at **www.raintreepublishers.co.uk** to browse our catalogue and order online.

First published in Great Britain by Raintree,
Halley Court, Jordan Hill, Oxford OX2 8EJ,
part of Harcourt Education.

Raintree is a registered trademark of Harcourt
Education Ltd.

© Harcourt Education Ltd 2008
First published in paperback 2008
The moral right of the proprietor has been asserted.

Editorial: Louise Galpine and Claire Throp
Design: Richard Parker and Tinstar Design
    www.tinstar.co.uk
Illustrations: Steve Weston, International Mapping
Picture Research: Mica Brancic
Production: Julie Carter

Originated by Modern Age
Printed and bound in China by Leo Paper Group

ISBN 978 1 4062 0766 8 (hardback)
12 11 10 09 08
10 9 8 7 6 5 4 3 2 1

ISBN 978 1 4062 0773 6 (paperback)
12 11 10 09 08
10 9 8 7 6 5 4 3 2 1

British Library Cataloguing in Publication Data
Moore, Heidi
Blood and celebration. – (Fusion)
299.7'92
A full catalogue record for this book is available from
the British Library

Acknowledgements
The publishers would like to thank the following for
permission to reproduce photographs: The Art Archive/
Bibliothèque de l'Assemblée Nationale Paris p. **24**
(Mireille Vautier); The Art Archive/Museo Franz Mayer
Mexico/Dagli Orti p. **23**; The Art Archive/National
Anthropological Museum Mexico/Dagli Orti pp. **6**, **18**,
22; Corbis pp. **27** (Danny Lehman), **28** (Franz-Marc
Frel); Corbis/Bettmann p. **12**; Getty Images/Stock
Montage/Hulton Archive p. **25**; Getty Images/Time
Life Pictures p. **26** (John Dominis); ©Museo Nacional
de Antropologia, Mexico City, Mexico/ Sean Sprague/
Mexicolore/The Bridgeman Art Library Nationality/
copyright status: Mexican/in copyright until 2063 p. **8**;
The Trustees of the British Museum [Scala, Florence]
p. **14**.

Cover photograph of turquoise mosaic of a
double-headed serpent reproduced with permission
of The Trustees of the British Museum.

Every effort has been made to contact copyright
holders of any material reproduced in this book. Any
omissions will be rectified in subsequent printings if
notice is given to the publishers.

The publishers would like to thank Nancy Harris and
Paul Steele for their assistance with the preparation of
this book.

Disclaimer
All the Internet addresses (URLs) given in this book
were valid at the time of going to press. However, due
to the dynamic nature of the Internet, some addresses
may have changed, or sites may have changed or
ceased to exist since publication. While the author and
publishers regret any inconvenience this may cause
readers, no responsibility for any such changes can be
accepted by either the author or the publishers.

It is recommended that adults supervise children on
the Internet.

This is a modern artist's idea of Huitzilopochtli. He is often shown wearing a feathered headdress.

Huitzilopochtli (say *weet-see-loh-pocht-lee*) was an important Aztec god. A god was a being people looked up to. He was often shown as a warrior. He carried a shield and weapon. His weapon was a **serpent** (large snake) that breathed fire. Huitzilopochtli's helmet was made of hummingbird feathers. His body and face were painted blue with white stripes.

The Aztecs worshipped Huitzilopochtli. They also feared him. Huitzilopochtli was a god of war. **Sacrifices** were made to him. A sacrifice is an act of giving up or killing something. This was done to please a god. War and sacrifice were important to the Aztecs.

Aztec gods

The Aztecs worshipped about 1,600 gods. They believed that the gods controlled their daily lives.

Some of the most important Aztec gods were:

- Coatlicue (say *co-aht-lee-cue*): Earth goddess and mother of Huitzilopochtli

- Quetzalcóatl (say *ket-zahl-co-ah-tul*): God whose name means "feathered **serpent**"

- Tlaloc (say *tlah-lock*): God of rain

- Tonatiuh (say *toh-nuh-tee-uh*): God of the Sun

- Chalchiuhtlicue (say *chal-che-oot-lee-cue*): Goddess of lakes and streams

- Tezcatlipoca (say *tehs-cah-tlee-poh-cah*): God connected to the darkness or the night.

Birth of a god

Huitzilopochtli's mother was called Coatlicue. The Aztecs believed Coatlicue already had a daughter. The daughter had 400 brothers and sisters: the stars. They were unhappy about Huitzilopochtli's birth. They planned to kill him. But Huitzilopochtli killed the daughter first. He cut off her head and threw it into the sky. It became the Moon. Huitzilopochtli defeated (beat) the night. He was then linked with the Sun.

reincarnate bring back to life

The Aztecs believed that Coatlicue (above) was Huitzilopochtli's mother.

The most important god was Huitzilopochtli. His name means "hummingbird warrior of the south". The Aztecs thought warriors were **reincarnated**. This means they were brought back to life. They thought they came back as hummingbirds.

Tenochtitlán

Huitzilopochtli had an important role. He was supposed to lead the Aztecs to their new city. At the time, the Aztecs were **nomadic**. This means they travelled from place to place. They never stayed in one place for very long.

In 1116 the Aztecs set off to find a new home. They were moving to the Valley of Mexico (see the map on page 4). They carried a picture of Huitzilopochtli. They believed he would lead the way.

The Aztecs built the city of Tenochtitlán. It was on the shores of Lake Texcoco.

nomadic   moving from place to place

The eagle was a sign that the Aztecs had found their home.

The Aztecs looked for the perfect home for more than 100 years. In 1325 they came to a large lake. An Aztec leader saw an eagle perched on a cactus. It was eating a snake. The Aztecs thought this must be a sign. Huitzilopochtli wanted them to live there! They decided to settle on an island in Lake Texcoco (see the map on page 4). They then built the great city of Tenochtitlán.

9

The Templo Mayor

By the late 1300s, Tenochtitlán was a big city. It had palaces and courts for ball games. It had a market and even a zoo. Thousands of people lived there. The most important building was the Templo Mayor. This means "great **temple**". A temple is a place of worship.

The Templo Mayor was a huge **pyramid**. It had triangle-shaped sides and a square bottom. It was built to honour Huitzilopochtli and Tlaloc. Tlaloc was the rain god. At the top of the pyramid were two temples (see page 11).

There was a **high priest** at the Templo Mayor. A high priest was a very important religious leader. He was called Quetzalcóatl Totec Tlamazqui. This name means "feathered **serpent** priest of our lord".

Play ball!

The Aztecs enjoyed playing a game with a rubber ball. It was played on a court called a *tlachtli*. One team would try to put the ball through the other team's goal.

high priest most important religious leader
pyramid structure with a square bottom and triangle-shaped sides
temple place of worship

This is what the Templo Mayor looked like in Aztec times.

Human sacrifices

Close to the Templo Mayor was a wooden rack. It had many human skulls on it. The human skulls belonged to **sacrifice** victims.

The Aztecs made sacrifices to their gods. These could be offerings of plants or animals. The most important gifts to the gods were human hearts and blood. Aztecs made human sacrifices to Huitzilopochtli. This was because he was linked with the Sun. The Aztecs believed that human gifts helped the Sun to shine. This helped the crops to grow. They also thought the sacrifice gave the Sun energy to move across the sky.

Blood sacrifice

Sacrifices took place at the Templo Mayor. They happened near the stone **altar**. An altar is a raised area. It is used for worship. A prisoner was taken to the **high priest**. The prisoner lay on the altar. The high priest cut open the prisoner's chest. He then removed his heart.

The Aztecs used a flint knife to cut out the heart of a sacrifice victim.

Festivals and parades

The Aztecs had many ceremonies. One was in honour of Huitzilopochtli. It was called *Panquetzaliztli*. Homes and trees were covered in paper banners.

Panquetzaliztli took place for three weeks. It was held in late autumn. During this time there were many **sacrifices**. There were parades and a race during the festival.

Near the end of the celebration, a huge **serpent** was burnt. It was burnt by priests. The large serpent was made of bark paper. This was paper made from the bark of trees. The serpent stood for Huitzilopochtli's weapon.

Aztec fact!

Panquetzaliztli means "the feast of the flags" or "the raising of the banners".

sculpture three-dimensional (not flat) art object, such as a carving or statue

Finally, the Aztecs cut up a **sculpture** of Huitzilopochtli. This statue was made of corn. They divided the corn among the priests and the young priests-in-training. The priests believed that eating this corn helped them. It gave them some of Huitzilopochtli's strength.

The blade of this knife is made from a type of stone. It is called quartz. Colourful stones have been used in the handle of the knife. The knife was used by the Aztecs for human sacrifices.

The Aztec calendar

The Aztecs had a calendar system. It was different from the one we use today. They had two calendars!

The first was a **solar calendar**. This was a calendar based on the movement of the Earth around the Sun. It was made up of 365 days. This calendar had 18 months. Each month was made up of 20 days. There were five extra days. The second calendar had only 260 days. It was made up of 20 signs and 13 numbers. This one was the **sacred** (holy) calendar.

Every 52 years the two calendars would match up. At that time the Aztecs had a huge festival. They also had a fire ceremony. First, they would let all their home fires burn out. Then, they would light a new fire. It was lit in the chest of a **sacrifice** victim. People thought the fire was sacred. They lit their torches from this fire. They used the fire to light their home fires. They believed it would bring them good luck.

sacred holy
solar calendar calendar based on the movement of the Earth around the Sun

This is an artwork of a painted calendar. The calendar is for 260 days. The calendar told the Aztecs when to do things. It could tell them when to plant crops or go to war.

Calendar stone

The calendar stone is also called the Stone of the Sun. At its centre is a picture of Tonatiuh, the Sun god. The stone shows the 20 days of the month. Each day is named after something important to the Aztecs. One of the days is called "Ollin", which means "movement".

The stone measures nearly 4 metres (13 feet) across. The days are labelled on the photo. Tonatiuh is also labelled.

Aztec days of the month

1 Crocodile – Cipactli
2 Flower – Xochitl
3 Rain – Quiahuitl
4 Flint – Tecpatl
5 Movement – Ollin
6 Vulture – Cozcacuauhtli
7 Eagle – Cuauhtle
8 Jaguar – Ocelotl
9 Cane – Acatl
10 Herb – Malinalli
11 Monkey – Ozomatli
12 Hairless Dog – Itzquintli
13 Water – Atl
14 Rabbit – Tochtli
15 Deer – Mazatl
16 Skull – Miquiztli
17 Snake – Coatl
18 Lizard – Cuetzpallin
19 House – Calli
20 Wind – Ehecatl
21 Tonatiuh, the Sun god

The Aztec Empire

At one point the Aztec **tribe** (group) was one of the strongest in central Mexico (see map). This was in the early 1400s. The Aztecs had **conquered** (taken over) many other tribes in battle. They took the tribes' land.

All the land taken by the Aztecs became known as the Aztec **Empire**. An empire is a large area of land. The land is under the control of one group.

By 1519 there were about 5 million people living in the Aztec Empire. It spread across 207,000 square kilometres (80,000 square miles).

Aztec fact!

The Aztecs thought their tribe was strong for a special reason. They believed Huitzilopochtli had blessed them. To keep the god happy, they made more sacrifices to Huitzilopochtli.

conquer take over by force
empire large area of land, or many lands, under the control of one ruler or group
tribe close-knit group
tribute money or goods given in exchange for protection

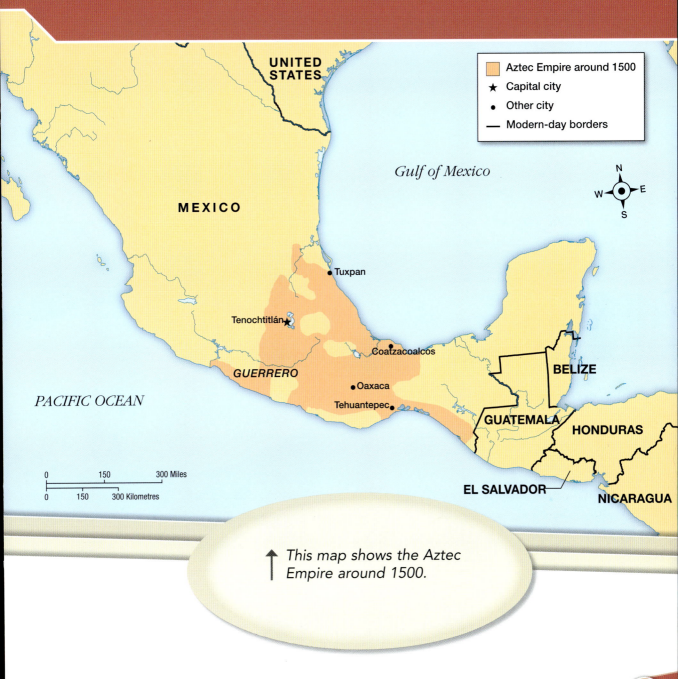

This map shows the Aztec Empire around 1500.

The Aztecs forced the conquered tribes to pay **tribute** to them. This meant that the other tribes had to give them goods and crops. These tribes also supplied many **sacrifice** victims!

Moctezuma

In 1502 a new Aztec ruler took over. His name was Moctezuma. You may have also heard him called Montezuma.

His people called him *huey tlatoani*. This is from the ancient Aztec language of Nahuatl. It means "great lord" or "great speaker".

This large stone is known as Moctezuma's throne. There are pictures cut into the stone.

This is how artists living in the 1600s think Moctezuma may have looked.

The Aztec **Empire** got bigger under Moctezuma's leadership. Tenochtitlán grew even more powerful. But this did not last very long. Things were about to change for Moctezuma – and for the entire Aztec Empire.

Cortés

In 1519 Hernán Cortés arrived on Aztec land. He was a Spanish **explorer**. An explorer travels through new lands. He brought with him an army of **conquistadors**. The conquistadors were Spanish soldiers. They helped Cortés take over Central and South America (see the map on page 21).

Cortés took over the Aztec Empire.

conquistador Spanish soldier who helped the Spanish explorer Cortés
explorer person who travels through new lands

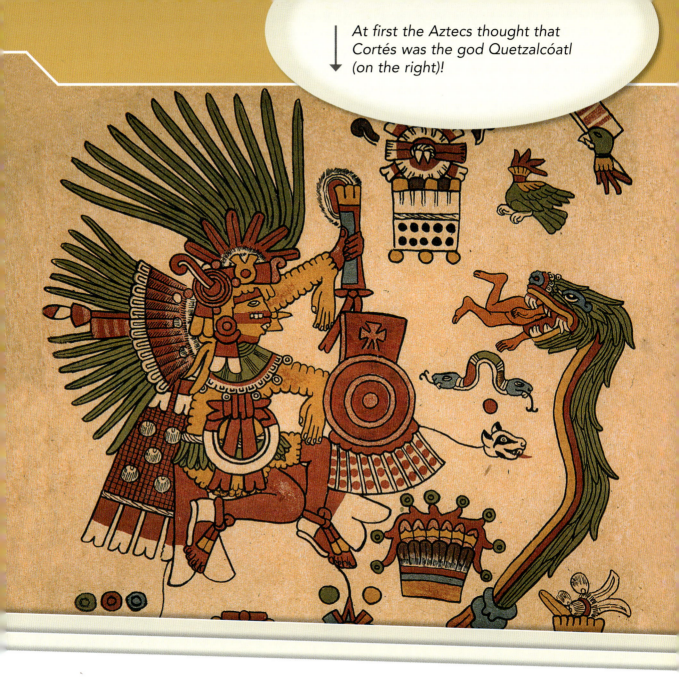

At first the Aztecs thought that Cortés was the god Quetzalcóatl (on the right)!

Cortés and his men took over the land quickly. We are not sure how they did this. We know they made agreements with certain **tribes**. These groups of people were unhappy. They had been **conquered** (taken over) by the Aztecs. They did not want to pay to support the Aztec **Empire**. These tribes helped the Spanish conquerors gain power over the Aztecs.

End of an Empire

Cortés and the **conquistadors** (Spanish soldiers) took Moctezuma prisoner. This happened in 1520. On 1 July he was killed. It might have been Cortés who killed him. Or perhaps it was Moctezuma's own people. They were angry about the Spanish invasion. We cannot be sure. No records were kept.

This eagle warrior statue was found near the Templo Mayor.

Ruins of the Templo Mayor can be seen in Mexico City today.

Soon after Moctezuma's death, the conquistadors began battling the Aztecs. The Spanish wanted control of the land. Within just a few years, the Aztec **Empire** was no more.

After that things changed. The Spanish did not believe in the Aztec religion. They did not worship Huitzilopochtli. They did not worship any of the other Aztec gods. They became Christians. They followed the teachings of Jesus Christ. Human **sacrifice** ended. A new way of life took over in the area. Eventually the area became known as Mexico.

Aztec beliefs live on

Today, the Aztecs are gone. But you can still see the remains of the Aztec **Empire** in Mexico. The Mexican capital is called Mexico City. It was built where the city of Tenochtitlán once stood.

Archaeologists are people who study the remains of past cultures. Archaeologists are still digging in the Valley of Mexico. They continue to find objects that once belonged to the Aztecs. More than one million Mexicans still speak the ancient Aztec language, Nahuatl.

A huge cathedral stands near where the Templo Mayor once stood.

archaeologist   person who finds out about the past
emperor   ruler of an empire

Timeline

AD

1325
Tenochtitlán is built.

1427
Tenochtitlán joins forces with smaller cities called Tlacopan and Texcoco. Beginning of Aztec Empire.

1431
Main **temple** (Templo Mayor) at Tenochtitlán enlarged. Empire expands.

1445
Ruler Moctezuma I expands Aztec Empire. Receives **tribute** from **conquered** peoples.

1454
More construction on Templo Mayor.

1473
Tenochtitlán conquers Tlatelolco to its north. Two cities combine, covering an area of 13 square kilometres (5 square miles).

1486
Aztec leader Ahuizotl conquers people in modern-day Guerrero and Oaxaca, Mexico.

1487
Large numbers of prisoners taken to Tenochtitlán for **sacrifice**.

1490
About 200,000 people live in Tenochtitlán.

1502
Moctezuma II crowned **emperor** (ruler of an empire).

1519
Cortés lands and is met by Moctezuma's followers.

1520
Moctezuma taken prisoner by Cortés's troops and then killed.

1521
Spanish (along with Aztec enemies the Tlaxcalans) take over Tenochtitlán and kill thousands. Last emperor, Cuauhtémoc, taken prisoner. City destroyed. Aztec Empire ends.

Glossary

altar raised structure or place that is used as a centre of worship. The Aztec priest stood next to the altar.

archaeologist person who finds out about the past. An archaeologist does this by digging under ground in places where people used to live many years ago.

conquer take over by force. The Spanish explorer Cortés and his forces conquered the Aztec Empire.

conquistador Spanish soldier who helped the Spanish explorer Cortés. The conquistadors formed agreements with local people to defeat the Aztecs.

emperor ruler of an empire. The last Aztec emperor was Cuauhtémoc.

empire large area of land, or many lands, under the control of one ruler or group. The Aztec Empire ruled for many years.

explorer person who travels through new lands. Spanish explorers went to Aztec lands.

high priest most important religious leader. The high priest stood on the Templo Mayor.

nomadic moving from place to place. Before settling in Tenochtitlán, the Aztecs were nomadic.

pyramid structure with a square bottom and triangle-shaped sides. The Templo Mayor was shaped like a pyramid.

reincarnate bring back to life. The Aztecs believed warriors were reincarnated as hummingbirds.

sacred holy. The Aztecs had a solar calendar and a sacred calendar.

sacrifice give up or kill something, often to please a god. The Aztecs gave sacrifices to please Huitzilopochtli.

sculpture three-dimensional (not flat) art object, such as a carving or statue. Aztec temples had many sculptures.

serpent large snake. The serpent was an important figure for the Aztecs.

solar calendar calendar based on the movement of the Earth around the Sun. The Aztecs used a solar calendar and a special holy calendar.

temple place of worship. The Templo Mayor was the most important Aztec temple.

tribe close-knit group. Many tribes lived alongside the Aztecs.

tribute money or goods given in exchange for protection. Other tribes had to give crops to the Aztecs.

Want to know more?

Books to read

The Aztecs, Penny Bateman (British Museum Activity Books, 1999)

Eyewitness Guides: Aztec, Inca, and Maya, Elizabeth Baquedano (Dorling Kindersley, 2005)

You Wouldn't Want to Be an Aztec Sacrifice!, Fiona MacDonald (Franklin Watts, 2001)

Websites

http://www.pbs.org/wnet/nature/spirits/html/body_aztec.html
You can learn much more about the Aztecs on this website.

http://www.pbs.org/conquistadors/cortes/cortes_a00.html
On this site you can read more about Cortés and the Aztecs.

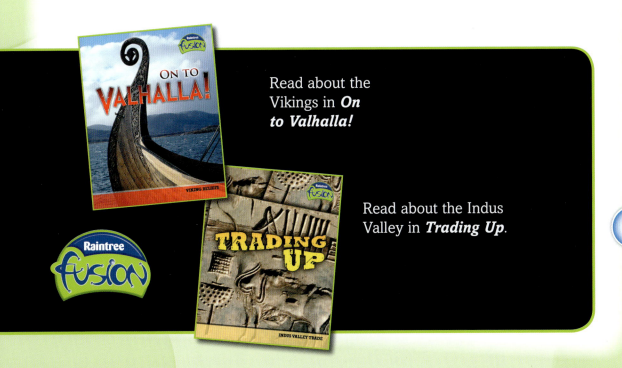

Read about the Vikings in *On to Valhalla!*

Read about the Indus Valley in *Trading Up*.

Index